THE DEEPENING STREAM
Poems of the Spirit — II

Life Reflections
of a Quaker in Retirement

By
Errol T. Elliott

With Cover Design and
Illustrations by

Dee M. Connett

Printed by
Prinit Press
Dublin, Indiana

Printed in U.S.A.
by
Prinit Press

CONTENTS

To the
New generation of Friends, worldwide,
in whose care a new chapter of the
Quaker movement will be written.

THE DEEPENING STREAM

Most of my life, especially in the recent half-century, has been involved in the life and faith of the people called Quakers. I have known them "separated" in their outward structure, but one in depth — a depth destined to surface in a new era of life and fellowship. It is from that awareness that I have been led to write, often objectively in prose, but ultimately from a depth of experience in which only the medium of poetry could suffice. The finer delineations of thought I leave to our theologians and philosophers.

Poetry, transcending all "isms" such as Quakerism, seeks to express the eternal within the temporal, from a depth known in the Christian-Quaker life and faith, born originally not in Fenny Drayton or on Pendle Hill in Northern England, but in Bethlehem of Judea, and being re-born in the Christian Churches today.

In the busy days of involvement one is drawn left and right on the horizontal level of action, though having the continual awareness of a central purpose. In retirement the level of action recedes and the depth dimension inevitably rises as the main concern. In a very real sense my later years have felt like a "deepening stream" that gives the title to this volume.

The present generation of Friends and their creative services are exciting to me. I sit somewhat as a "fan" observing the thinking and action and rejoice in what I see. History is never so interesting or so important as when it comes as a fulfillment of the life and thought of a people, such as the people called Quakers. If the movement is "of the life" it will call for new patterns that meet the needs of mankind.

The new generation of Friends is responding, blending the past-present with the unfolding future of Quaker life and faith.

GRATEFULLY

I am especially indebted to Dee Connett, Associate Professor of Art in Friends University, for her interpretation of what I have written, through the medium of art.

Only one person can write the poem, but many persons can support and inspire the poet. Many friends have thereby helped to produce this volume. The continuing concern and correspondence with Jack Willcuts, Superintendent of Northwest Yearly Meeting of Friends, and editor of the *Evangelical Friend*; the empathetic fellowship of Kara Cole and Jack Kirk as secretaries and writers in the expanding services of the Friends United Meeting; the fellowship of University Friends Meeting in Wichita, with its pastoral team of David Kingrey, Dorlan and Donna Bales; and my fellow retirees at Prairie Homestead — these experiences with friends and Friends are of the fellowship in which my life in recent years has been immersed.

The memory of Friends and events, as reflected in part in my *Quakers on the American Frontier* has been a deeply moving incentive for writing, earlier in *prose* and now in *poetry*. The Friends United Meeting, the Friends World Committee, the establishing of Quaker Hill as a Conference Center, and the Earlham School of Religion are major movements of Friends with which I have been closely associated and which give confidence for the future.

As I turn my memory pages the ministry of the late Everett Cattell, whose clarity and depth of life has blest Friends far and near, rises at a new turn in the history of Friends. Many others could be included one by one.

More personal still was the daily support and service of Evelyn Clark Elliott, whose flair for order and accuracy and whose preparation of the final manuscript made the production possible.

E. T. E.

OF PROSE AND POETRY

In a deepening sense the mind and pen of man moves from prose to poetry, from closely reasoned form to depth of experience. The Bible is replete with examples.

The apostle Paul broke through the restraints of his carefully written prose and "sang" his faith and experience in his canticle to love (I Cor. 13).

The psalmist, in the great poetic section of the Bible, is not *analyzing* life, he is *experiencing* it at its depth-center and poetry is his natural way of telling it, a medium closely related to the other arts, music and painting.

It requires both prose and poetry to express fully mind and spirit within the wholeness of life.

POETRY AND COMMUNION

It has been said that poetry was what Milton saw as he went blind. His insight was sharpened as his sight was dimmed.

For some persons poetry is what they hear as they become deaf. Conversation gives way to the flow of sound as words dim out and communion becomes the better part of communication.

Such is the deeper language of poetry.

THE FIRST DIMENSION
A Prayer

Thou, Lord of Life: Help us to keep open the depths of our lives as we face the daily activities that draw us left and right. Thou art the Source from whom we live and move and have our being, known so fully in the life of the Man of Galilee. Give us the patience to live by the words of the Psalmist: *Wait, wait I say, on the Lord!*

SPIRITUAL PRIORITIES

Inwardness,
    then Outwardness;
Insight,
    then Foresight;
Communion,
    then Communication;
Experience,
    then Explanation;
Wisdom,
    then Courage;
Love,
    then Service.

MEMORY

Thou mystery of mysteries — the mind
Within whose secret folds reside the years;
Cascade of childhood's tumbling thoughts, the fears,
Youth's lavish dreams, with ventures ill-designed,

Yet deep within on upward course inclined,
Discernment, sense of values then appears;
The finest of the yesterdays endears
And in maturing thought become refined.

From creeping fears of aging now recoil;
Strange resurrection as on lilting wing,
From sum of years with Tennyson I sing:
Old age hath yet his honor and his toil.

In fullness of the years to live again,
And fill the unwrit page I take my pen.

TOWARD THE ETERNAL

In mind of man, in death, in birth
Thy light breaks through with heaven on earth

THOU ART!

In Search
Who art thou, Lord,
    who will not let me rest
    until I rest in Thee,
    and in that rest
    to seek thy will
    and find my own —
    reborn!

Art Thou —
    My burning wayside bush
    that Moses knew,
    which turns my steps
    to thy people
    in distress?

    The voice that commands
    as through Balaam's beast,
    to stop my wilful way?

    The still small voice
    of Elijah's cave,
    that calls to depth
    beyond all sight and sound
    and tumults of the world
    and sends me, reassured,
    upon my way —
    made thine?

In Truth
Thou art in Truth
    the Presence in the midst
    that speaks to each, to all,
    the two or three, or many,
    to make us one in spirit
    and tempers well our zeal;
    that sends us forth
    committed to Thy mission
    that the gates of hell
    cannot withstand!

Within the mystery of Life,
    beyond the problem
    is the Presence
    inviting, inspiring, commanding;
    the ultimate affirmation —
        Thou Art!

CHRIST IN PENTECOST

You ask me whence I came and where I go,
But when I come as Presence you shall know.

O THOU ETERNAL
A Hymn

O Depth profound from whom we came,
Unfolding ages laud Thy name;
The centuries formed of years and days
Call forth our voice to sing Thy praise.

O Height unscaled in whom we rise,
We trace Thy path in swarming skies;
As morning stars in chorus sing
Our lives and hope to Thee we bring.

O Thou Eternal, One in all,
We tune our spirit to Thy call;
Thy presence moves in star and clod;
As loving Spirit Thou art God.

O Depth of soul where Thou art known,
Thy inward voice from zone to zone
Inspires the dream in every land
For Thy design, Thy kingdom planned.

O life revealed in Galilee,
Our lives we bring and yield to Thee;
Thy light makes clear our common day,
Thou art in Christ, the Truth, the Way.

THE EVER PRESENT

Time
    that was,
    that is,
    that shall be;
This I know within,
    the ever Present.
In this awareness is
    my assurance,
    my heritage,
    being revealed,
    discovered.
This, the Eternal
    from whom
    life unfolds;
    to whom
    it infolds,
    in communion.
Seen in Christ,
    incarnate in time,
    inwardly known,
    in whom life centers,
    from whom life springs—
    the ever invading Presence,

THOU HEAVEN — — —

What eyes and ears and hands have known,
Thou, heaven that art and yet shall be,
We visioned in the skies far flown;
Not strange that we so pictured thee!

We laid thy streets with burnished gold,
Mined from the depths of western hills
And naught withheld of wealth untold
Our largesse from refining mills.

We mined quartz layers of the earth
To shape and build thy jasper walls,
Bedecked with gems of rarest worth
Thy splendored irridescent halls.

We swept the shell beds of the seas
To build and swing thy gates of pearl,
Adorned replete o'er wall and frieze
With jewels, amethyst and beryl.

We built thy throne of dazzling white,
The best earth's quarry yields
To give thy streets eternal light
That floods o'er thy Elysian fields.

– – – ON EARTH

Yet, building we have failed to see
In earth and sky thy artistry,
The cloud flotillas floating by,
The liquid gold of evening sky;

The bracing strength of winters bare,
Like blades of ice the cutting air;
The birth of Spring, an April morn,
The fulness of a year reborn;

The resurrection on the earth
When death is lost in vast rebirth;
In petal, leaf we failed to see
And trace their lacy filigree.

For beauty these could not suffice,
But love that shines through sacrifice
In saintly lives of charm and grace;
Serenity in an aged face.

We read the wisdom of the sage
That truth is truth in every age;
In mind of man, in death, in birth
Thy light breaks through with heaven on earth.

RESPONSE

Ye meek take heart, there is no evil chill
That can restrain the power of Love, of Will

AWAKENING

Ah, crowded sky,
    alive in movement,
    changing, unfolding;
    replete with galaxies,
    stars in death and birth!

What cosmic guide,
    tethers of law,
    hold you in orbit
    around some central Sun?

As part of creation
    I stand awed,
    trembling,
    akin to this swarming night.

The whisper
    that spoke creations word
    speaks now to me
    as to a star;
    calls to communion.

Touch my dull clay
    that I may live,
    respond, listen silently,
    as if from some far sphere
    a little child
    would sing to me!

SPRING SONG

Like dawn, Spring trembles on the eastern rim,
As if to venture on a day unknown;
Lord of the sky the solar orb newblown
Begins with cadence of a distant hymn.
The first faint notes awaken latent tones,
Responses from each root that feels the stir
Of life, the newborn flower, fresh flow of myrrh —
The incense from the blossoming field. The stones
Now feel the lifting soil, the power of light.
The sun, to lead the chorus of the earth,
Now summons forth his host in vast rebirth
To sing that death is dead, that Life is might!

Ye meek take heart, there is no evil chill
That can restrain the power of Love, of Will.

PRAIRIE REFLECTIONS

Come, walk with me across the open plain,
    push back the tall bluestem, brush ankle-deep
    with the first new blades of Summer,
This time-made garden, untouched by man,
    invites each plant to be its own.
The carpet of grass,
    food for the buffalo that left its name,
    spreads everywhere under all, through all;
    its texture, made brittle by winter frost,
    answers to our every step.
Here the dandelion,
    enemy of city lawns, finds welcome
    with its lavished gold.
The cactus leaf
    offers its desert fruit,
    red prickly pears.
Prairie daisies in a sequestered nook
    lift petals, blue and white on short slender stems,
    to drink the sun.
The locust clings to a swaying stem
    and sings his solo, as if it matters only
    that God should hear.
Small creatures
    whose homes are in the soil,
    colonize, burrow and build earth homes,
    now scurry around us;
    the gopher who knows more than he will tell
    of earth layers left by many years
    lifts his mound.
The coyote scents the elusive hare,
    then in evening shadows
    sits baying at the moon.

Here the drama of survival,
        on a stage that Darwin never knew,
        is played — the hunter and his prey.
The prairie dog fortifies his home
        with a mound of earth;
        lord of his castle he sits at his door,
        chatters with his neighbors
        and scolds all intruders.
Here is the world of flight:
        prairie chickens, quails, and doves
        rise on a whirr of wings;
        the hawk soars low
        ready to dive and take his prey;
        the prairie owl sits blinking at the sun,
        the meadow lark trills as if the world
        is made for song.
This wild Eden must pass away;
        the farmer and the plow will come
        and a June sea of wheat will wave
        where little wild things once made their homes;
        the world must be fed, but an inward pang
        strikes deeply as we turn homeward.
Indeed, must the time come
        when there is no wild prairie
        on which you and I can walk
        with primal thoughts
        on the eternal and the changing,
        what was, is and yet to be?
A bleak emptiness comes within,
        to be relieved only by the memory of
        the living prairie —
        the lost Eden!

MOUNTAIN SUNSET

Here, deep in valley shades,
Eyes up, soul out,
I wait . . . .
The rapture holds.
Hills spired in flint against the sky
Etch a gothic line from South to North —
Strange graph rising to mark the mind's ascent
Upward, upward toward the sun, till
One shaft strikes farther, sharper than the rest,
Then the master of the day,
Full orbed, earth pierced,
Can hold no more his pent up bounty
And across cloud islands
Explodes in liquid flames.

IN LIGHTER VEIN

Within our serious concerns there must
also be a ripple of humor, of pleasure,
of empathy with our common experiences
if we are to find wholeness, living both
seriously and lightly toward life.

HOMESTEAD EDEN

We wake each morn to hear, to see
Our own Homestead Menagerie
Of crows and doves, and busy grackles,
Whose voices range from coos to cackles;
The sparrows with their happy twitter
Building nests and making litter;
The swallow glides on tilted wing,
In perfect grace, when does she sing?
To anyone who tunes his ear
The cardinal sings, *Good Cheer! Good Cheer!*
Of all God's creatures seen or heard
There's nothing like the mockingbird;
From tips of trees her heart afire,
All by herself a feathered choir,
With songs of birds both great and small
Her repertoire — she sings them all!

To fellowship and friendly talk
The paths invite our daily walk
Across the bridge, the castle moat,
Where leaves of water lilies float,
Whose buds explode in petaled flames
And gold fish play their water games.
The pool becomes our inland sea
That turns our minds to Galilee.

Each patio a homeside shrine,
With cool fresh air like bracing wine;
The fluffy islands floating by
Like woolly sheep across the sky;
The flaming gold of evening sun,
The art supreme when day is done.

THE KILLDEER FAMILY

You came to us as welcome guests;
Beneath what bushes were your nests?
Where was your home and where your eggs
That turned to chicks with spindly legs?
We find our language short of words
To welcome you, dear little birds.
Mom spreads her wings around each one
Protecting you from rain and sun;
She calls you in for safety chats,
"Beware, beware of dogs and cats!"
Forever make our lawn your home,
But wheresoever you may roam
You"ll sometime sing when we're not near;
It is enough that God should hear,
So sing, sing on, *"Killdeer, Kildeer"*.

RESIDENTS IN FLIGHT

Wild ducks from some far southern break:
We welcome you to Homestead lake;
You come to us on winds that blow
To Canada from Mexico.

Are you tame, or are you wild?
You ask for food much like a child,
We try to see that you're well fed
With corn and seeds and crumbs of bread.

From warming Spring to chilling Fall
You must obey your inward call
To flight for some far northern brink,
'Tween South and North as living link.

The time will come when you must fly;
With inward pain we'll say goodbye.
We know that you are birds of flight,
That some One guides you day and night.

LIFE AND TRUTH

So this is life, to hazard and to gain,
In which the giving is its own reward.

LURE OF TRUTH

We sense the boundless freedom of the skies;
Our spirits soaring like a bird in flight
From depth within that answers unto height,
For knowledge that our thought can but surmise.
    Thou art the restless urge within the mind;
    Thy velvet fingers twine the strands of thought
    By which the fabric of our life is wrought,
    As Thou the silent Weaver hast designed.
Thy truth comes not across a vast abyss,
Nor with the trumpet's sound or earthly din,
But as a breath, a whisper from within,
Like winged beauty breaking chrysalis.
    The flowering bud youth opened to the Sun,
    Now feels the depth of truth, as day is done.

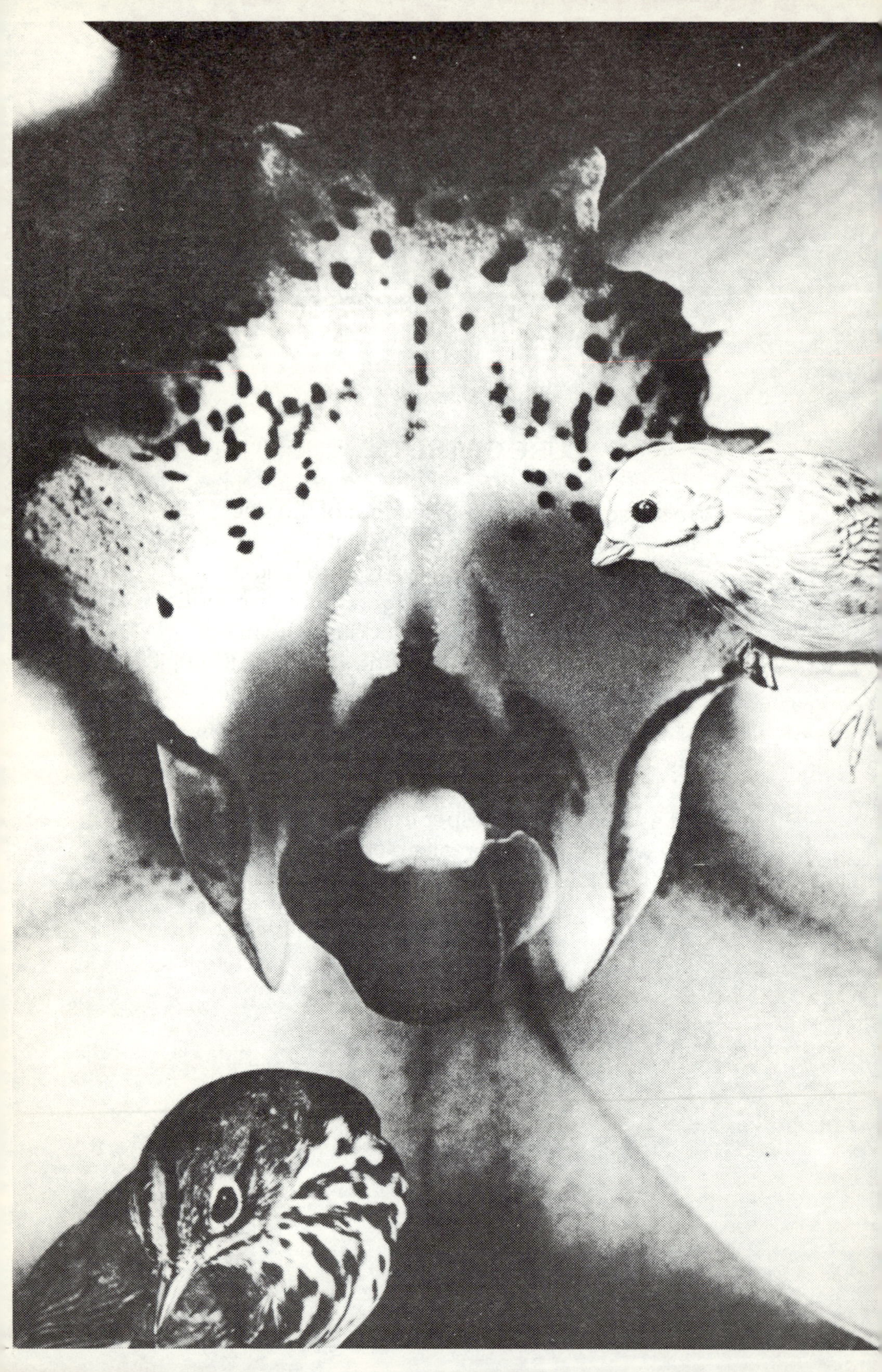

A LIFE UNMEASURED

We cannot measure yonder spring
By cupfulls from its laughing rill,
Or hold the glint of redbird's wing,
Or frame the song of whip-poor-will.
There is no measure of a man,
We only see a life unfurled,
And life is timeless, not a span
Within our metric-minded world.
He sees the parts that make the whole,
Would lift his world toward God entire,
Within it he accepts his role;
His conscience a celestial fire.
From added years beyond his youth
And depth of insight he can rise
With flash of wit to speak the truth;
His is the humor of the wise,
He is a living prophecy:
A man committed to his call,
Who lives for that which ought to be,
On human skyline standing tall!

THE PROPHET

Who is this prophet, this far ranging man
With depth of insight, scope of mind to think,
Between the earth and God as living link
Discerns the future, draws it into plan.
    What are those silent fingers of his mind,
    That probe a peoples history immense
    To write its lessons in the future tense —
    The loom on which their history is twined.
From spirit depth his vital faith is grown,
Live currents flow to thaw the frozen creeds;
Release the power of faith in living deeds
Conceived in thought, but first in spirit known.
    Creative mind whose vision is unfurled;
    Like hands of God he helps man shape his world!

REVELATIONS

Like thistledown caught from a passing breeze,
A vagrant seed takes root within the mind
For test in life, by thought to be refined,
In hunger lure truth only can appease.
    When comes the call as if to lofty quest,
    One ventures forth to hazard and to dare
    And climbing fills his thoughts like mountain air,
    For some majestic truth, some Alpine crest.
Or comes a truth as with a burst of light,
Like lightning's flash that rives a darkened earth,
Full blown to live, begot in holy birth,
As living thought leaps from the depth of night.
    So came the quest root-deep when life began,
    So answers man to God and God to man.

PARADOX

Think twice and thrice where great thoughts intersect,
Escape the dead-end trap of either-or,
With sharpened mind strike there for richer ore;
From deeper source truth rises tall, erect.
    Heed well the voice from Galilean shore:
    Give, lose your life that Life indeed might be,
    Then you shall know the truth that sets men free;
    That all they lose, in turn, love will restore.
So this is Life, to hazard and to gain,
In which the giving is its own reward,
And love renews what self and greed had marred;
Then Life for all is lived from deeper vein.
    It is not sacrifice one's self to give,
    If in the giving he has learned to live!

THE LIVING CHURCH

Frail temple in the unabating storm,
Our fingers trace to feel your trembling lines,
Your tottering walls — these but the worldly signs
To test the structure in its outward form.
>But this is not the Church, this but its frame;
>Like ancient forests upward grew its beams
>As pillars, rooted in deep running streams
>In depth to live, in spirit more than name.
We do not go to quarried pits for stone,
Nor to the flaming forge for tempered steel
To build your temple by our human zeal,
But to the depths of man, in every zone.
>As giant redwoods rive the fertile sod
>For living streams, their branches feed the sky,
>The Church arises, links the deep, the high
>To be the living temple of our God.

OF FAITH AND TRUST

Till *every* mortal stroke of tongue or pen
In one response may sing, *Amen! Amen!*

A TEACHER'S PRAYER

Thou Mentor of the mind, the soul,
From inward call to outward role,
Inspire my search, invade my thought
That as I teach I may be taught.

Not in the books that line the shelf,
But from the depth within the self
Be in our thought as living link
From what we know to how we think.

In interplay of mind with mind,
In deeper search for richer find
Of truth that comes through doubtings rife,
Help each to answer with his life.

Teach us to know that truth is might
Implanted as our inward light,
And give us true insight to see
The bottom line — integrity!

AT TIMBERLINE

Rage ye storms,
    assail my flesh bare limbs,
    fling far my needle leaves;
    my roots ye cannot touch.

I dare your
    thunder rains,
    lightnings lash, gales
    that can but hymn
    heroic praise
    to life that will not yield.

My purpose holds
    in veined roots thrust deep
    within arterial streams,
    from which creation sprang
    in drama ages gone.

I strike beneath
    time-sculptured rocks,
    upthrust from depth
    a million million years
    when earth, convulsed,
    was being formed;
    before they were, Life was.

On timberline came
    Socrates,
    Joan of Arc,
    Martin Luther,
    Lincoln;
    supremely, the Galilean;
    all who
    with integrity
    dared to live!

THIRD BIRTH

Winged from the realm of spirit as in flight
We enter first our world of sound and sight
Within the loving care, the frills, the lace,
That frame the wonder of a baby's face.
    Midst things and thoughts we start our lifelong quest,
    Discern the good, the better, and the best;
    In growing learn to choose in terms of worth,
    And in commitment come to second birth.
In flow of life to love, to gain, to give
And know at last, we have begun to live
Till span 'tween earth and heaven is but a breath —
How strange, in passing, we should call it death.
    So moves our inward spiral on the earth;
    Then morning breaks in third and wondrous birth!

THE INWARD CROSS

Ah Anguish, I had heard afar your name,
But knew you not until at last you came
Into my spirit depth a piercing blade,
Till time with prayer and thought my pain allayed.

As if within a throng I heard a cry,
Jesus of Nazareth is passing by!
And from within the crucible of grief,
Refined by fire he gave new faith, belief.

Life is not reckoned simply gain or loss,
In love he bears with us the inward cross,
And from the spirit depth and inner strife
There comes in final test new birth, new life.

Within the time of stress life is revealed;
Beyond the saving cross our wounds are healed.

THE GREAT AMEN

In one consuming passion of all time
We try to frame the one uniting word,
Or join in quest for an elusive chord
That brings a world of discord into rhyme.
     Of all man's latent hungers this is prime —
     To shatter now and ever spear and sword
     In dawn of universal peace out-poured,
     With harmony to every race and clime.
The answer comes not only with our charts
But as, off stage, and waiting in the wings
An organ plays; a distant chorus sings
And brings to symphony our diverse parts
     Till every mortal stroke of tongue or pen
     In one response may sing, *Amen! Amen!*

THE POEM

On the breath of spirit,
    a whisper,
    wordless,
    free flowing
    comes the thought,
    half-articulate.

The search for form,
    a frame of words
    to discipline the thought.

Language responds,
    bends to its task,
    to shape the words,
    to form the verse;
    from communion
    to communication —
    the poem is born.

The form must pass,
    leaving only
    the universal,
    the quest for life
    from which it came.

The poet passes,
        leaving but an echo
        of life as he knew it —
        an echo time will dim,
        but never end;
        the form, the poet
        are expendable,
        the spirit-depth, never;
        others will catch the echo,
        and write
        from the endless wonder.
The poem is forever!